FACT PLANET

POLLUTION

IZZI HOWELL

Franklin Watts
First published in Great Britain in 2020 by the Watts Publishing Group
Copyright © the Watts Publishing Group 2020

Produced for Franklin Watts by
White-Thomson Publishing Ltd
www.wtpub.co.uk

Series Editor: Izzi Howell
Series Designer: Rocket Design (East Anglia) Ltd

HB ISBN: 978 1 4451 6905 7
PB ISBN: 978 1 4451 6906 4

All **bold** words appear in the glossary on page 30.

Getty: cinoby 10t, Artis777 16t, Robert Pleško 17t, 2Xena 21tl, UnitoneVector 22t; Shutterstock: BlueRingMedia cover, MuchMania title page and 6t, grmarc 3t and 18t, Pogorelova Olga 3b and 17b, vectorpouch 4t, Denis Belitsky 4b and 28t, Eduard Radu 5t and 30, Tivanova 5bl, Kev Gregory 5br, Maja81 6b, Delpixel 7t, Hung Chung Chih 7bl, VioNetta 7br and 28c, WindAwake 8t, trgrowth 8b, prochasson Frederic 9l, LMIMAGES 9r, Krasula 10b, Zentangle 11t, Maike Hildebrandt 11c, Ondrej Prosicky 11b and 28b, VectorMine 12t, Mary Terriberry 12b, Tanor 13t, Laurence Gough 13b, VectorPot 14t, Martchan 14b, Chepko Danil Vitalevich 15tl, Damsea 15tr and 29t, N.Savranska 15b, Rich Carey 16b, Spreadthesign 18b, riza azhari 19tl, Libor Píška 19tr and 29c, Hannes Mallaun 19b, randy andy 21t, Sarah Fields Photography 21b, SlyBrowney 21tr, Julia's Art 21b, Elizaveta Galitckaia 22bl, kanvag 22br, Mountain Brothers 23l, Orakunya 23r, Hal_P 24t, curiosity 24b, brown32 25t, Funtap 25bl, Nadin Panina 25br and 29bl, Kastoluza 26t, NotionPic 26b, Shebeko 27tl, yanik88 27tr, Nikola Bilic 27b and 29br.

All facts and statistics were correct at the time of press.

Printed in Dubai

MIX
Paper from responsible sources
FSC® C104740
FSC
www.fsc.org

Franklin Watts
An imprint of
Hachette Children's Group
Part of the Watts Publishing Group
Carmelite House
50 Victoria Embankment
London EC4Y 0DZ

An Hachette UK Company
www.hachette.co.uk
www.franklinwatts.co.uk

Find the answers to all questions in this book on page 28.

Contents

What is pollution?

Pollution is damage done to the environment by people.

There are many different types of pollution. Factories, power plants and vehicles release poisonous gases into the air. This is known as air pollution. Water pollution is rubbish and waste that is dumped into rivers and oceans.

PICTURE PUZZLE

This machine produces lots of air and noise pollution. What is it?

Dumping waste and chemicals on land can poison the soil and make it hard for plants to grow there. Noisy roads, factories and airports create noise pollution (pages 18–19) and too much **artificial** light leads to light pollution (pages 20–21).

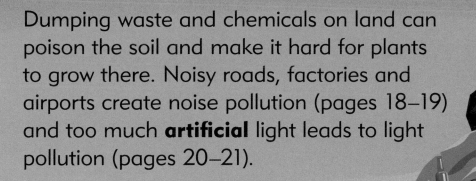

FACT!

4.2 million

people are killed every year by diseases linked to outdoor air pollution.

Pollution hurts the natural world. It poisons and kills plants and wild animals, which affects the entire **ecosystem**. It also damages human health. For example, people can develop lung disease from breathing lots of polluted air.

Animals can get trapped and hurt in rubbish (see page 16).

Air pollution

Air pollution comes from factories, power plants and vehicles.

In many power plants, **fossil fuels**, such as coal, oil and gas, are burned to **generate** electricity. This process also produces air pollution. Vehicle exhausts and factories are also sources of air pollution.

Air pollution contains tiny **particles** of chemicals that hurt the internal organs, such as the lungs and the heart, when they enter the body. This can cause health problems, such as **asthma**, and serious diseases, such as lung and heart disease and cancer.

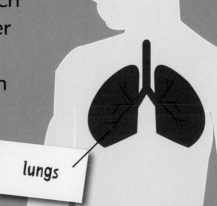

lungs

There are other ways to produce electricity that don't create air pollution, such as wind turbines. The spinning movement of the turbine's sails in the wind generates electricity without burning any fuels or creating any pollution.

9 out of 10 people around the world breathe polluted air.

 PICTURE PUZZLE

This is another way of generating electricity without air pollution. What is it?

The greenhouse effect

Some gases make the temperature on Earth hotter.

Air pollution contains **greenhouse gases**, such as carbon dioxide and methane. These gases cause the **greenhouse effect**, which makes the temperature on Earth rise.

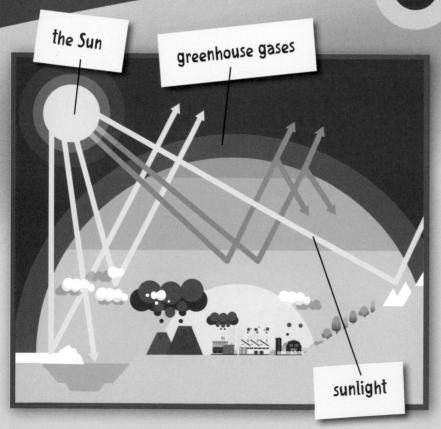

the Sun

greenhouse gases

sunlight

Greenhouse gases gather in the air around Earth. They trap heat from sunlight close to Earth's surface so that it can't travel back into space. This makes Earth hotter, which is also known as **global warming**.

QUESTION TIME

WHAT IS THE NAME FOR THE LAYER OF GASES THAT SURROUNDS EARTH?

a Aerosol

b Atmosphere

c Meterology

Greenhouse gases are also released naturally. Humans and animals breathe out carbon dioxide. Volcanoes release greenhouse gases when they erupt. Natural levels of greenhouse gases keep Earth warm enough for living things to survive. However, greenhouse gases from air pollution are making the temperature rise too high.

FACT!

Cows produce methane, a greenhouse gas, when they burp and fart!

water vapour and carbon dioxide breathed out

Climate change

Global warming is changing Earth's weather.

The rising temperatures on Earth are leading to **climate change**. Places around the world are experiencing much hotter and much colder weather than usual. Heavy rain and **extreme** storms are becoming more common.

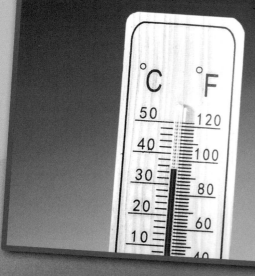

FACT!

The five years from 2014 to 2018 were the hottest years ever recorded.

Climate change affects people in many ways. It is hard to live in very hot or cold places. Bad weather and **drought** are killing **crops**, so there isn't enough food in some areas. Heavy rain and storms cause flooding, which damages people's homes.

Climate change also affects wildlife. The ice at the poles is melting in the warmer weather, destroying the habitat of polar animals, such as polar bears. Many plants are being killed by the extreme weather, which means that there is less food and shelter for animals.

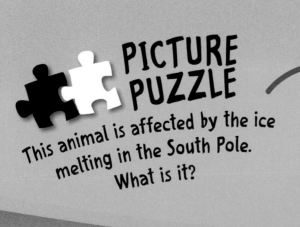

PICTURE PUZZLE

This animal is affected by the ice melting in the South Pole. What is it?

Acid rain

Air pollution leads to acid rain.

Some chemicals from air pollution mix with water and oxygen in the air. They form acids, which can fall to the ground as acid rain or snow.

acid rain

acid snow

water vapour (gas)

air pollution

When acid rain lands on trees and plants, it damages them and poisons the soil. Some acid rain falls into rivers and lakes and pollutes them. The acid hurts or kills animals that eat affected plants or live in polluted water.

QUESTION TIME

WHICH OF THESE LIQUIDS IS AN ACID?

a Lemon juice

b Milk

c Water

Acid rain is sometimes carried across large distances by the wind. It falls in areas that are far away from the source of air pollution. This can make it hard to work out what is causing the acid rain.

The ears of this statue have been dissolved by acid rain!

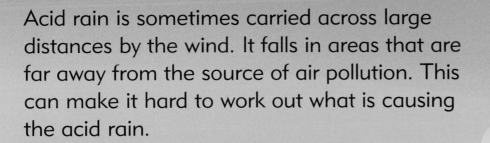

Acid rain dissolves anything made from limestone, including buildings and statues!

Water pollution
Chemicals and waste pollute rivers and oceans.

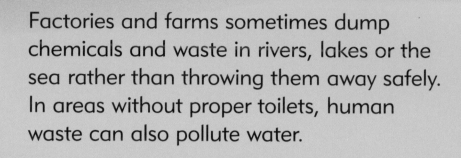

Factories and farms sometimes dump chemicals and waste in rivers, lakes or the sea rather than throwing them away safely. In areas without proper toilets, human waste can also pollute water.

Polluted water poisons the animals and plants that live in it. Some animals or plants may die because of this. This affects water ecosystems. If lots of one species die, this affects the other animals that depend on them for food. Humans can also get sick from drinking polluted water.

Some areas in less economically developed countries don't have any safe sources of drinking water. People have to drink from polluted lakes and rivers, which makes them ill.

One in three people around the world does not have access to safe drinking water.

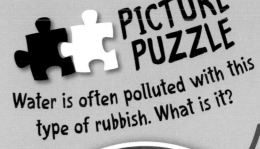

PICTURE PUZZLE

Water is often polluted with this type of rubbish. What is it?

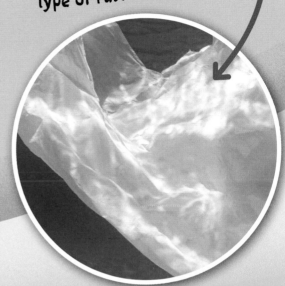

The best way to reduce water pollution is for the government to stop businesses dumping waste into water. Ask your local politician what they are doing to help keep your local rivers, lakes and seas clean. You could also join a community group that helps to protect these spaces.

VOLUNTEER

VOLUNTEER

Ocean rubbish

Pollution in the ocean hurts animals.

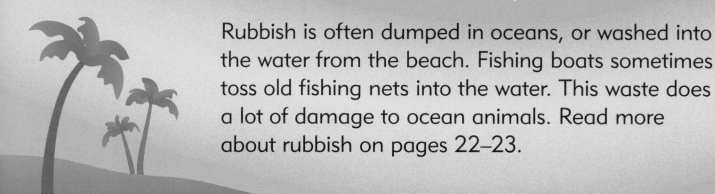

Rubbish is often dumped in oceans, or washed into the water from the beach. Fishing boats sometimes toss old fishing nets into the water. This waste does a lot of damage to ocean animals. Read more about rubbish on pages 22–23.

QUESTION TIME

WHERE IS MOST OCEAN POLLUTION CREATED?

a) Fishing boats

b) On land

c) Cruise ships

Ocean animals can get trapped in large pieces of plastic or fishing nets. This hurts them. Trapped animals can sometimes drown underwater. Some animals confuse rubbish for food. When they eat rubbish, it damages their insides and can kill them.

Scientists think that 9 out of 10 seabirds have plastic in their stomachs.

Oil spills are another threat to the ocean. Oil leaks into the water from ships or **oil rigs** and covers ocean animals. Oil-covered animals can't move properly or keep warm. When they try to clean themselves, they eat the oil, which poisons them.

Noise pollution

Too much noise can harm animals and people.

Factories, airports, roads, ships and construction all produce large amounts of noise. This may not seem like a big problem, but over a long period of time, this repeated noise harms people and animals living nearby.

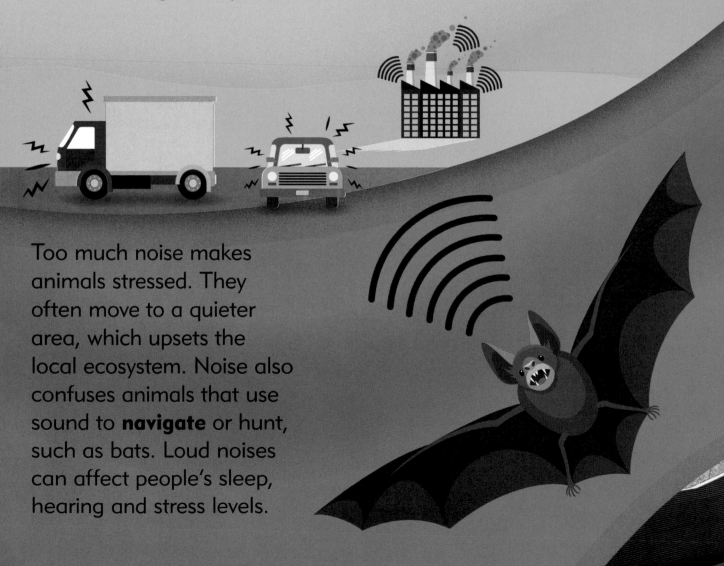

Too much noise makes animals stressed. They often move to a quieter area, which upsets the local ecosystem. Noise also confuses animals that use sound to **navigate** or hunt, such as bats. Loud noises can affect people's sleep, hearing and stress levels.

Noise pollution can confuse whales so that they get trapped on beaches and die.

The government can help bring down noise pollution by making laws to reduce noise. New roads and airports should be built away from houses and animal habitats. Walls can also be built around noisy places to block the sound.

PICTURE PUZZLE

This object helps to protect your hearing from loud noises. What is it?

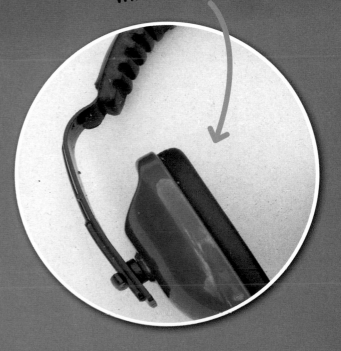

Light pollution

Light pollution makes the night less dark.

Light pollution comes from homes and businesses that leave their lights on at night. It happens most often in towns and cities, where lots of individual lights combine together to make a lot of light pollution.

FACT!

The light pollution from the city of Las Vegas, USA, can be seen from nearly **150 km away!**

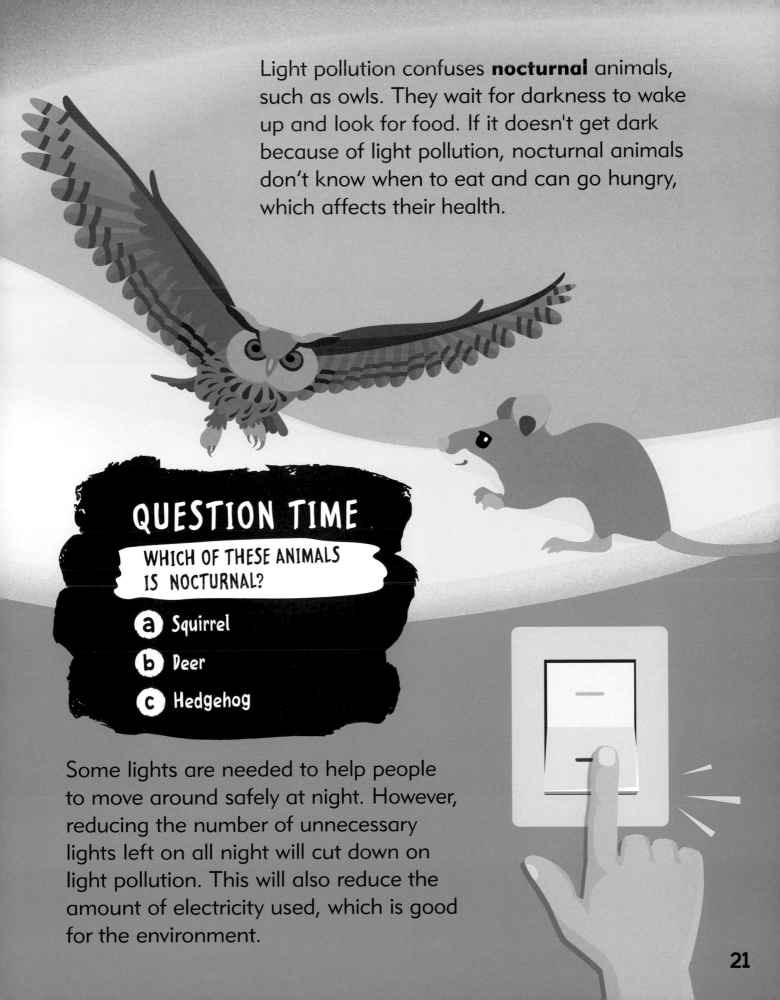

Light pollution confuses **nocturnal** animals, such as owls. They wait for darkness to wake up and look for food. If it doesn't get dark because of light pollution, nocturnal animals don't know when to eat and can go hungry, which affects their health.

QUESTION TIME

WHICH OF THESE ANIMALS IS NOCTURNAL?

a Squirrel

b Deer

c Hedgehog

Some lights are needed to help people to move around safely at night. However, reducing the number of unnecessary lights left on all night will cut down on light pollution. This will also reduce the amount of electricity used, which is good for the environment.

Rubbish

Most of the rubbish that we create becomes pollution.

When we throw something in the bin, it is collected and usually taken to a landfill site. This is a hole in the ground where rubbish is buried. Sometimes chemicals from the rubbish leak out of the landfill site and poison the soil around it.

Most of the rubbish that we throw away is not **biodegradable**. It will not break down for hundreds or even thousands of years. As time goes by, we are filling up more and more space with landfill sites. Eventually, we will run out of room for more.

FACT!

The world produces over **3 million** tonnes of plastic and solid waste every day.

Some rubbish is biodegradable, such as leftover food or scraps, such as peel or cores. This can be made into compost in a compost bin. When added to soil, compost helps plants to grow well. Food waste is collected from homes in some areas to be composted. Check if you can take part.

QUESTION TIME

WHICH OF THESE MATERIALS IS BIODEGRADABLE?

a Wood

b Plastic

c Metal

Reduce, reuse, recycle

Creating less rubbish helps the environment!

Producing less rubbish means that fewer landfill sites are needed. We can reduce the amount of rubbish we create by buying fewer objects and avoiding unnecessary packaging.

Reusing items also helps to cut down on rubbish. Try to reuse items as much as possible before throwing them away. For example, you can wash up and reuse plastic cups and reuse scrap paper for writing or drawing. Look for second-hand clothes, books or toys.

Many materials can be recycled, rather than thrown away. They include glass, aluminium, paper, cardboard and some types of plastic. However, recycling does require energy, which can be polluting. So try to reduce or reuse before recycling.

FACT!

Making cans from recycled aluminium uses 95 per cent less energy than making them with new aluminium!

PICTURE PUZZLE

These objects can be recycled in special bins. What are they?

Cleaning up

We all have a part to play in reducing and cleaning up pollution.

Factories and big companies release most of the pollution around the world. They have the most important role to play in cutting down pollution, but they don't always do so. However, we can show these companies that we want them to change. For example, we can stop buying from companies that create lots of pollution or start a petition.

Governments can also help reduce pollution by making rules that companies have to follow, such as the amount of pollution they can release. Find out what your local politician is doing to help stand against pollution. If they could be doing more, send them an email and ask them to help.

Helping to save the environment from pollution can feel like a huge job, but if we all do a little bit, it makes a big difference. Try making small changes, such as walking, cycling or using public transport rather than going by car. Use reusable containers, bags and cutlery rather than disposable ones.

FACT!

A **million** plastic bottles are bought around the world every minute!

PICTURE PUZZLE

Washing with this helps to reduce plastic waste. What is it?

Answers

PAGE 4

Picture Puzzle:
An aeroplane

PAGE 7

Picture Puzzle:
A solar panel

PAGE 9

Question Time:
b) Atmosphere

PAGE 11

Picture Puzzle: A penguin

PAGE 12

Question Time:
a) Lemon juice

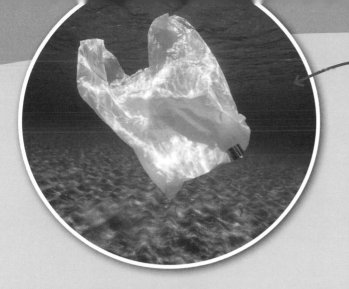

Glossary

artificial not natural

asthma a medical condition that makes it difficult to breathe

biodegradable describes something that breaks down naturally without harming the soil

climate change changes to the weather on Earth

crops plants that are grown in large amounts for food

dissolve when a solid becomes part of a liquid

drought a period of time when there isn't enough water because not enough rain falls

ecosystem all the living things in an area

extreme unusual or very serious

fossil fuel a fuel that comes from the ground, such as coal, oil or gas

generate to produce or make

global warming the increase of the average temperature on Earth

greenhouse effect the increase in temperature on Earth caused by greenhouse gases being trapped in the atmosphere

greenhouse gas a gas, such as carbon dioxide, that traps heat in the atmosphere

navigate to find the right direction to travel

nocturnal describes an animal that is active at night

oil rig a structure that is used to remove oil from under the ground, often at sea

particle a very small piece of something

Further information

Books

Go Green
by Liz Gogerly and Miguel Sanchez (Franklin Watts, 2019)

Plastic Planet
by Georgia Amson-Bradshaw (Franklin Watts, 2019)

Pollution (Ecographics)
by Izzi Howell (Franklin Watts, 2019)

Reduce, Reuse, Recycle (Putting the Planet First)
by Rebecca Rissman (Wayland, 2018)

Websites

www.bbc.co.uk/newsround/47148382
Take a quiz about pollution around the world.

climatekids.nasa.gov/air-pollution/
Learn more about air pollution.

your.caerphilly.gov.uk/kidsgogreen/fun-zone/rubbish-challenge
Play the Rubbish Challenge and see which items should be
reduced or recycled.

Index